How Our
Bodies Learned

"Marilyn Kallet's poems burst with the dark sound of Lorca's *duende* as they travel through time from Tennessee to France and back again. The ghosts of beloved poets, family histories, and the animal inside us haunt this collection, constantly clawing at the page. Heart-rich and stunning, the poet traverses tragedy at home and abroad, both the personal body and the body politic, toggling between ode and elegy. Kallet prepares a prosodic feast for the reader's senses with her words and performance. This is an unctuous book stuffed with luscious obsessions: of words and love and lust, which conjure Dante and desire, the muse of our flesh and bone. Here is an intersection between the sacred and the sexual, of pain, pleasure, loneliness, and departure. These musical, muscular poems praise the darkness, blessing the broken world with humor, truth, and delight. If poems are bodies that remind us of our bodies, then Kallet's somatic poems tackle what it means to be alive and dazzling.

—Tiana Clark, author of *Equilibrium*, winner of the 2016 Academy of American Poets University Prize. Her poetry appears in *The New Yorker* and *American Poetry Review*.

How Our Bodies Learned

POEMS BY

MARILYN KALLET

Black Widow Press is an imprint of Commonwealth Books, Inc., Boston, MA. Distributed to the trade by NBN (National Book Network) throughout North America, Canada, and the U.K. All Black Widow Press books are printed on acid-free paper, and glued into bindings. Black Widow Press and its logo are registered trademarks of Commonwealth Books, Inc.

Joseph S. Phillips and Susan J. Wood, Ph.D., Publishers
www.blackwidowpress.com

Cover Art: *Emerging* by Agnes Carbrey, 2014–16, Oil on Canvas, 24 x 36 inches. agnes.carbrey@gmail.com

Design & production: Kerrie L. Kemperman

ISBN-13: 978-0-9971725-4-6

Printed in the United States
10 9 8 7 6 5 4 3 2 1

ACKNOWLEDGMENTS

Some of the following poems have appeared or are forthcoming in magazines and anthologies. Grateful acknowledgement is made to the editors.

"Kitchen Rag," "Old Sun," "What I Never Had," *Bluestem*

"Paris Elegy," "What Will Baby Eat?" *Blue Lyra Review*

"Ode to My Shawl," "Encore," *Asheville Poetry Review*

"Ode to Late Autumn," "Before After," "Ode to Solitude," "Turn Back," "Often," *Plume*

"Ode to Disappointment," "On Loving Two Men at Once," "Doctor Knows the Blues," "What a Pilgrim Needs," *Plume Anthology of Poetry*

"What Power Has Love?" *J Journal: New Writing on Justice*

"My Downward Dog," "Passionate," "Losing It," *Connotation: An Online Artifact*

"Falling Out," *War, Literature, & the Arts*

"What I Never Had," "Old Sun," *Potomac Review*

"Splitting, Auvillar," "Ode to a Petal on the Riverbank," *2 Bridges Review*

"Ode to the Handsome Frenchman," "Longest Night," *Ray's Road Review*

"Retreat," *Iodine Poetry Journal*

"More Like Me," *One*

"Dream Witness," *New Millennium Writings*

"Big Love," *Jewish Currents*

"Moth Light," *Still: the Journal*

"Out" was first published in *Ironwood*, then in *In the Great Night*, Ithaca House, 1981.

"Warrior Song," *Truth to Power: Writers Respond to the Rhetoric of Hate and Fear*, published by *Cutthroat, A Journal of the Arts*.

"Wake Me (After Orlando)," collaborative poem with Benjamin McClendon, on Leslie Tate's blog.

"Anti-bullet Adult," *Black Heart Magazine*

"Anti-bullet, #2" and "Anti-bullet, #3," *Woven Tales Press*

"Praise," "Hard Love," "How Our Bodies Learned About Flint" (early version), *In God's Hand*
"Eden Again," *SynoptIQ*
"Muse," *The Phoenix*

Many thanks to my publisher Joe Phillips at Black Widow Press for encouraging my poetry and translations over the years, and to Kerrie Kemperman, graphic designer and copy editor at Black Widow Press. To the Virginia Center for the Creative Arts and its offshoot, VCCA-France in Auvillar, where many of these poems were written. Sheila Pleasants is the deputy director of artists' services at VCCA in Virginia; she was a prime mover for the spectacular VCCA-France.

The village of Auvillar is home to pilgrims, muses, friends: Lucy Anderton and Jean-Philipe Roux, Nigel and Christine Macallister, Odette Barratto, Claude and Raymonde Dassonville, Anne-Marie and Francis Brune—each year they welcome us, poetry pilgrims. VCCA-France director Cheryl Fortier and her husband John Alexander keep the workshop and the poets humming. Photographer and chef Christophe Gardner teaches poets to taste and see. Nanie and Daniel at Galerie Arts' Kad open their doors and wine bottles for poetry readings. Chef Francis Comte and his journalist spouse, Jo, offer delicious hospitality. Olwin Fleming stands ready with Scotch when pollen steals my voice before a performance. Agnes Carbrey, visionary painter, teaches at James Madison University and in Auvillar; her swimmer (*Emerging*) graces the cover of this volume.

Thanks to my friends Vincent, Dominique, Dénis and Lucy at Hotel Quartier Latin, for watching over me during the Paris attacks in November, 2015. Thanks to Marilyn Hacker, Jennifer Dick, Margo Berdeshevsky and Sandy Anderson for camaraderie during the worst of times, and to Shakespeare and Company for hosting us at the Paris reading in 2016. Cheers to Daniel Lawless at *Plume*,

Keith Flynn at *Asheville Poetry Review*, Julie Brooks Barbour at *Connotation* and Mathew Silverman at *Blue Lyra Review* for welcoming the Paris poems.

Thanks to Brother Bob Baxter and Mount St. Francis in Indiana, where poetry and spirit meet. To sister writers Barbara Bogue, Deborah Harper Bono and Alice Friman. To my sister Elaine Zimmerman, whose poetry and public service inspire.

Thanks to the English Department at the University of Tennessee, to the Hodges Fund and to EPPE (Exhibit, Performance, and Publication) at the College of Arts and Sciences; these have generously funded travel and expenses related to my books. I am grateful to my colleagues, Allen Dunn, Stan Garner, Charles Maland, Amy Elias, Mike Lofaro, Arthur Smith, Margaret Lazarus Dean and Joy Harjo, my sister spirit. Thanks to Liam Hysjulien, Cameron Molchan, Kali Meister and Andrew Dillon for performance practice, bourbon and critiques. Thanks to the undergraduates who created a memorial booklet of poems for Zaevion Dobson's mother, Zenobia, and to Zenobia Dobson, for attending our memorial reading. To Richard Faussett, *New York Times* Atlanta Bureau Chief, who also attended the memorial reading at the university, and wrote about it, May 4, 2016. Thanks to the anonymous facilities worker who rescued drafts of the Zaevion booklet from the office recycle bin and left me a note about their beauty.

I am grateful to Randall Brown at the *Knoxville News Sentinel*, Todd Steed, Regina Dean, Victor Agreda, and former colleague Matt Schafer Powell at WUOT. Local Channel 8 has aired segments on poetry; thanks especially to Donovan Long, Amanda Harra, Ted Hall and former reporter Kyle Warnke. Thanks to Tearsa Smith at WATE 6, "On Your Side." Margaret Renkl at Humanities Tennessee faithfully showcases Tennessee authors in the newsletter, *Chapter 16*. My friend Tomi Wiley James successfully promoted Poetry Spring in Knoxville.

The Knoxville Writers' Guild is a friend to poetry; so is Flossie McNabb at Union Ave. Books. Tristan Charles at Parnassus in Nashville makes our books available at the Southern Festival. Serenity Gerbman herds us poetry cats each year. Thanks also to Leslie LaChance and the Global Education Center in Nashville for hosting me.

Taryn Norman deserves praise for her work with domestic abuse victims in Tulsa and thanks for inviting my poetry to be part of the healing. I am grateful to San Bernardino Police Chief Burguan for his service to North Park Elementary, and for his encouragement of my work. And to Benjamin McClendon, for collaborating with me on "Wake Me, After Orlando." Grateful to British author Leslie Tate, for showcasing our poem and my essay, "Poetry in Times of Crisis," on his blog.

Always thankful to my friend and editor Dr. Julia Demmin. Over the decades she has carefully read everything I have written.

Love to my husband, Lou Gross, who married poetry when he married me, and to my daughter Heather Gross, who sets a standard for editors.

CONTENTS

I. After Eden

II. Turn Back

III. How Our Bodies Learned

What power has love but forgiveness?

—William Carlos Williams,
"Asphodel, That Greeny Flower"

I. *After Eden*

KITCHEN RAG

Que dire de celles qui pourchassent l'obscurité avec leur torchon...
(Vénus Khoury-Ghata)

What to say of those who hunt shadows with a dishrag? Me,
I purchase chicken soup, add garlic, noodles, wine.

If not enlightenment, tradition. I inhale *poulet* perfume
and the healing art of some phantom Jewish mother

who alchemized poultry. Someone's *Yiddishe* mama stirred that pot,
if not my Southern mom. If I inhale vapors of chicken,

l'chayim stirs me. Though poems adore the flavor of obscurity,
they will not thrive there, not in Villon's freezing attic, nor in poor

Baudelaire's. Someone with humid breath must be reading them,
strolling through the village with a volume of Lamartine under an arm,

or hunched inside ancient walls with her laptop stealing wi fi—then
her songs have half a chance of being born, finding someone

else's eyes. Not Rimbaud's, those of another young poet
who yearns to escape his tidy village, military parades,

grizzled vets and Girl Guides. He will transport my verses like a torch
into Paris, into his thoughts and heart, into his well-toned body.

That's another *histoire.* For the moment,
chicken soup begs to simmer, and I will not leave the gas lit

without striking a match. Back off, Sylvia!
Too late to die young, pointless to

towel down ragged,

                        indifferent shades.

ODE TO LATE AUTUMN, AUVILLAR
(November 4, 2015)

Yellow leaves and green river
Do not add up to song,

Do not console.
But this is not a song about

Not-having. There's a blackbird
In gold leaves

And the bare top branches
Gleam redder

Than my lipstick.
Bluebirds sweep

From tree to tree.
Something in them knows

What's coming.
They don't name it winter

Or absence. They don't moan
About missing you.

What they need they fly toward,
Like me.

If you'll have me,
We'll take the long way home.

PARIS ELEGY

On Rue Bichat
on the shattered street
you want a poem

for Friday.
I have only
words

that hang heavy
in the air
like church bells.

129.
129.
129.

Notre Dame
stays locked
until Thursday.

A precaution,
you understand.
Words?

I have Sunday
blue sky above
the Seine,

police boats
and foot patrols,
grumpy tourists

who "came all this way"
and can't enter
la Chapelle.

I have one family
at home
in Tennessee,

another here,
in Paris,
smaller now,

reduced to long echoes,
130
low sounds.

(*Paris*, 11/15/2015; 11/18/2015)

ODE TO MY SHAWL
(November 15, 2015)

Soft ivory,
you held me,
my little wrap,

sheltered me
in Paris
while I wept.

My husband
trembled overseas.
Mon amie ancienne

drew down her
sullen
veil—

"Not the time
for poetry."
No? Gentle cloak,

you warmed me.
Humans
left me cold.

BEFORE AFTER
      (Auvillar, November 5)

    1.
The American poet tumbled hard.
Idiot tried to slam second-floor shutters
without Mister Long Arm.

The American died of flesh-eating bacteria,
wringing ancient sponges in the
artist colony kitchen.

The American succumbed
during a long bilingual
poetry reading at the Galerie.

The American died of hippie hair
at Annie's chic salon.
Died again of shame

after the once-over
by lycée girls.
The American wasted away

after French grocers
refused to notice her.
The American expired

waiting for the washing machine,
though she had dialed *Éco-Rapide.*
There will be no services for the American.

No rabbi in Auvillar.
All the Jews were killed or hidden
during the war.

That's no way to end a funny poem,
Dante said.
O you should know, I said,

with your laugh-a-minute
chute to the inferno,
and your narrow stairway

up the gold-tipped road.

2.
What the Jewish comic
didn't dream was Bataclan,
blood on rue Bichat,

didn't fathom bombs.
People
torn.

Police boats, foot
patrols, machine guns
along the *jolie* Seine.

Notre Dame
no one's this week.
Locked. Métros closed.

"Our flight cancelled!"
Texans complained,
at the sidewalk café,

Rue Monge.
Maybe no way home.
Maybe 9/11, but

French.
All her fears
seem small now,

dated in the wake
of blasts,
129, 129,

130 carillons.
Unimagined,
What we have denied

to love
turns
wolf at the rim.

Too-human
monster.
The wolf inside.

(*Paris*, November 13–18)

ODE TO SOLITUDE

You are my shadow,
My second self,
My home,

Respite.
You are my loss,
My lack of.

Wrapped
Around my arms,
You are too big for me.

When I want sleep,
Too small.
Be my pillow,

Companion.
Take pity on me.
Dream in me.

Teach me how to be
More human
Without.

Lend me a new word
That means ghost-of-love.
I am enough,

And not enough.
Teach me
To love absence,

The idea of him
More than
The man.

MY DOWNWARD DOG

A is crumbling like an ancient wall in Cahors. "Don't you spot *ruines
partout?* Between forests and highways, between

you love me and
dead air.

Someone will climb. Someone will marry them.
How to marry a wall?

Or a letter. Start by pride-swallowing.
Like alphabet soup, all beginnings.

When your letters clog
the heap, go out for wine.

Marry a book. You're a writer.
Eat those words.

Note that A is still beautiful
while it crushes you.

A was loving at first.
Like reading the first book. *Goldilocks.*

Little bear burned by alphabet soup.
Like nothing else on earth,

crueler. A stone alone in the field.
Castle in the distance.

Too far to throw.

FALLING OUT

According to *Le Monde, désamour* reigns
between nations, which means
falling out of love,

Triptik
to forget it.
Dice your love

and make
a tapenade,
serve on hard toast.

I too have tried falling out,
my yearning
more rock wall

than slide.
Let's scale
down, baby-step back

to mere
crush.
Désamour.

Désamour mucho.
Can't say "Come back"
to never.

What does wind
know,
stripping limbs?

According to *Le Monde*
there has been a
decrescendo,

but in my dreams
your face is sharp—
foreground to infinity.

You are world,
mountains
waving *yoo-hoo*

to molehills,
nothing lost or gained.
In another country

you are no less beautiful,
at home in fierce
wind.

You live in me.
I translate your flesh
into words,

your beauty a touch less
ravaging
in song.

WHAT I NEVER HAD

I looked for you and carried you
        everywhere, my brother,
my poet-heart, my
exquisite
absence.
What could I reach, reacht
        As I was? Carted you
to the village in my heavy
valise, to the market in my
plastic *sac* with its black cat,
to the married cheeseman. I
transported you to the post office
and the foreign stamps, to the
pâté de campagne, to the stone
inside my mouth, to Madame's
roses and thorns,
letters, silences,
the cold bed.

One can go only so far with
absence, and I have gone so far,
taken you to the thunder
of cannons
that seeds the clouds,
gone
farther
on a glance
than anyone.
Except maybe Dante.
I carried him, too,
from shore to shore,
from the dead to the living.
Sometimes his rhymes assuaged my longing.
Sometimes.

SPLITTING, AUVILLAR

Madame Dassonville cups my face in her hands,
      "God will bless your journey.
He knows you love Him!"
        "Stupid cunt!" Two North-African men
curse me when I block narrow St. Pierre
      to load my bags.

Madame D's eyes gleam.
      "She knows!" my friend Lucy claims.
Yet I am stupid in the Hybrid.
      I do have a
cunt, though I'm not
      over-identified
      with it.

Maybe the men are railing,
      "Late for work again!
      Now we won't
      make rent and the
      stupid privileged
      American cunt
      stops to load more
      luggage than
      a human needs!"

Madame D. promises
      next time she will
drive me to Moissac, to the
      house that once hid Jews.
Nine years since
      we first met &
now she knows me
      well enough to
speak of war,
      les juifs,

French complicity. "You
        are my French family," I
say, and mean it. *"Mais oui!"*
        she clasps me, too hard.

        The angry dudes
have a point, too.
        "Pity the poor
immigrants" you & I
        once were, my
copains. Grandma Anna sweated
        out the wait
        on Ellis Island.

I should have said, "Forgive me,
        my brothers, I have slowed.
        I'm a worker, too,
        in words—back in the day
        I waited tables and
        shop counters,
        tended my
husband, baby,
the strays.

I am a clumsy hybrid between
        earth and *ailleurs,*
a mother like the one
you emerged from,

        who still cries missing you—
who blesses your journey
        over rough seas
and cold hearts,
        the one
who loves you
        without question."

ALCHEMY OF BODY AND VERB

> "...mad love, illusive love, miserable love,
> ecstatic love, gossipy love,
> love without name..." (Julia Kristeva)

Illusive I know best.
Elusive, too,

raised on clouds,
vowels,

hint of black hair.
Love without touch,

bias, basis.
Humble

poet love,
mad syllable love,

stubble love, brother
lost love, walking-away

love, come-back
love that has no hope

of love.
Dante without Bea.

Ancient young
no-middle-

ground
love, endless

preface
love, flickering

ashes love,
whisper

love
without name,

one name,
on my tongue.

WHAT WILL BABY EAT?

Baby will eat pâté
foie gras

caviar
fat tears

Baby will eat
blues

Coltrane &
Madeleine

Peroux   duck
breast

duck mousse,
Baby will eat

rillette
whipped

cream
crême

brulée
this little pinkie

dipped
in champagne

Baby will
nibble

you
down

to the
bone.

ODE TO THE HANDSOME FRENCHMAN WHO
WANTED TO BE YOU

He stared me down and claimed he wanted to be you.
He wanted your fervent eyes, your punch-drunk black hair,

Your pecs and abs your poetry your agile hands
Your fantasies your

No, I said, you cannot be my other.
You'll never be Dante.

Never my muse.
Sure, you made it into one poem but that's it, buddy.

The feature film has been cast.
D. transported me through hell and back,

not a hair on my head was singed.
You're glossy. But can you compete?

Can you croon your way past monsters on
both sides of I-75? Leap over

generations gaping between us in one
bound? You're a flame, sure,

but the real you, the prototype, is wildfire,
hillsides gone, ashes blown

away in a whisper.
One almost second-guesses

having been touched.

ON LOVING TWO MEN AT ONCE

Okay, three. The crooner
    young enough to be
my grandson—who am I,
    Georgia O'Keefe?
The second, son-like,
    son-down, and
bien sûr, my careless,
    dark-eyed
    husband. Whom I
adore. It's harmless, Ladies
    & Gents, long as
all comers remain
    locked in an ode.

While we're ensnared in
    dream light,
why not add the hotel owner's
    son at the Quartier Latin, my
tool-time hero with his
    homemade quickie cardboard boxes,
dark-haired Fabio
    tearing duct tape with
his teeth, while his toddler son,
    rapt, studies him.

On loving four men at once—
    N, S, E, W, and let me be
the center of the compass!
    It's part-time love, in a country
of lost souls and souvenirs,
    4/4 time.

Dark-eyed gentlemen
    of my dreams,
I'd say there are none

like thee among poets
with swift feet,
    but I just tagged a few more.

In the realm of perfect bodies
    & dream light,
of ordinary love,
    there's plenty
to go around,
    loop-de-loop.
Loup-de-loup.

"How do you say 'roller coaster'
    in French?" I asked.
"Les montagnes russes,"
    Fabio said.
"I love you like the
    Russian mountains—
up and down."

WHAT POWER HAS LOVE?

1.
Farmers fire cannons
at the clouds   to shatter hail

the egret
skittish   takes wing
                                       I tiptoe

                                       not all absence
                                       about you

2.
Le Monde
bears news of anti-Semitism
                        Farouk Hosni
wants to obliterate the money-grubbing Jews
he's up for Director General of Unesco

Ilan Halimi, 23,
a Jewish man tortured for weeks in Paris

stabbed, burned, murdered   27 people on trial
by a gang, the Barbarians   "Jews have lots of dough"

the French police
won't call it a hate crime

one cannot lock every door

3.
"What power has love but forgiveness?"
my daughter is lean and strong like the egret

her blonde hair may go back
to some German ancestor

she works for an American newspaper
in a town where the governor's hair

disqualified him for a reality show
soon she will write about our travels

to Barcelona
if we can find the city

but we are two strong competent women
with one fine GPS

4.
Chaumage
last week's vocabulary word
means unemployment

really means it.
In Spain more than 38 per cent

of people Heather's age
are out of work

robbery is up
we make copies of our credit cards

5.
Today's word, *coqueluche*,
"whooping cough"

applied to a young princess
means the talk of the town

not every word is a metaphor
if it were, we might apply this   to the Brit next door
                                           who tore off her clothes

                                           and flashed the guy at the café
                                           terrace
he had peered down on her
in their garden

invaded her privacy
so she invaded his   enraged

now their house
and prize roses are for sale

6.
Not every word
but many

how can I miss   what I never had

Eden   no mosquitoes?

but here   they are the size of hummingbirds

and slow,

slow,

not every object is beautiful

not every space charged   with longing
sweetheart

7.
Wanted to write about "the presence of love,
not its pursuit"
wanted to

means my daughter,
my husband,
my friends—
let absence turn
to morning light that reveals the egret
and compassion for Ilan's mother, whose
son was the age of my daughter

not the pursuit, the kind that chatters and runs circles
wants to evade fear
le coeur au creux des reins

Not a hate crime?
Love harder then.

II. *Turn Back*

TURN BACK

"Intergenerational sex is a trend," Jeannine said.
"But how many generations can we skip back?"

"That's grotesque," Bill spat.
He should know. Long ago, that thing

with the teen. Who gets residuals from that?
Not Jan, she's middle-aged by now.

We can joke all we want but I was ready to
to stop the count.

Then I summoned my daughter's wedding.
Won't skip that.

I'm trying to articulate hunger that
hollows a person out. "Cannibalize yourself,"

Clayton Eshleman advised. If I'm already
bones, what then?

Turn back to Dante, a voice said.
he's the one man

who asks
directions.

DOCTOR KNOWS THE BLUES

"There are worse things than fried pie," Lou says.
"Like what?"
"Like fried Ding Dongs, fried Moon Pies."

Last night at the Bijou Lou urged me to say hello
to the Barry, the mandolin player,
throwback to forty years ago.

I was, as my mother would have said, "shacking up"
with Barry's roommate, the lead singer.
We were screamers.

I'm sure that's what Mr.
Mandolin remembers.
That we kept the boys up.

They wanted to be us.
We wanted to be us,
until we didn't.

"Don't do anything
you don't want the whole world
to know about!" my mother used to say.

Too late, Ma.
Let the Circle Be
Unbroken, forty years

down the line, or smash it
to bits
when the band

plays Dorsey's "Doctor Gonna Fix It,"
and I try to beg off, "We were not friends,
Mr. Mandolin and I."

Lou insists, "But you were there!"
There are worse things
than fried pie.

I can't speak of them, even now,
not to Lou. Not to a poem.
Little deaths. Then real ones.

WHAT A PILGRIM NEEDS

"A pilgrim needs only the Bible!" hails the "Welcome" folder
at the friary house.
Wish they'd told me sooner. I would not have schlepped

Rilke, Neruda, *Lumina* literary mag,
Joyce Maynard, Polizzotti's life of André Breton.
I triaged my mascara — a Jewish girl's

retreat. I'm packing *Packing Light, Circe, How to
Get Heat.* "I'm going to Hell!"
Brother Bob says. He cursed the Creator during

Sunday night's sleet. March, and the
mount shivers, grasses are sere.
No lilies greet frogs at the lake.

The braided postal lady displays
Jimi Hendrix and hard hat
commemorative stamps:

Build America! Fine.
Or build a life in song.
Where's Corso?

Ginsberg?
Maxine Kumin?
Anne and Sylvia, guess not.

No Rimbaud and Verlaine,
no *amours de tigre* at the Mount.
Emily's cameo has been done.

Pilgrim, they say all you need is the Bible.
Still, great stripper stamps might sell—
Gypsy Rose Lee,

Blaze Starr,
Magic Mike.
Had we but script enough,

our looks,
ten million bucks,
and time.

RETREAT

Sister Rose planned to talk to teens about the Holy Ghost. The
boys of Saint X hid in the back parking lot, jerking off.

You morphed into my phantom, nothing into something.
My refrain, my incantation. Every bluish moon

you would show in the flesh, utter a word,
leave trace evidence.

Love, our subject.
We women prayed to it and *baked it like bread.*

I would have done whatever it took.
Faith and madness slap each other on the back,

old buddies in my liturgy of you.
Unholy thought: do you throb when I

cry out your name? I worship what I have, distance
between us, rural road map turned illuminated book.

Sister Rose has her hands full of hormones.
So do you, from your unsaintly look.

You mystery, you test of my inner life,
my outer life,

my marriage. More holy shit
than holy ghost.

You saw that coming.

ODE TO DISAPPOINTMENT

"Dear Marilyn,
The committee has decided
not to fund your Professional Development
proposal. We think you are already developed.
Other applications have risen to the top,
like chicken fat on cooling soup.
Other applicants may be newer,
less developed, but more promising,
more professional. Poetry
is not professional. Poetry sits alone in a dark
room and who knows what it does?
We suspect it touches itself.
You don't need a grant to write poetry.
All you need is a pen and a bottle.
Cheap swill. Think Bukowski,
We never offered him a dime.
Or Keats. We did not fund him. He mined his own
sources. You can find your own cash. Your husband,
for example, got the best raise ever this year,
because he scares us. We don't mean he's violent,
just that he never shuts up and his criticisms
are professionally developed. So go home and
sleep with your rich dick, we mean your spouse.
See how that works out. We have faith in your
ability to surmount us."

THE DEATH OF ROMANTICISM

Dennis was random, a six-night stand,
long-haired well-built dude, who
        dug ditches, patched roads.
Romanticized poets, poor
guy. Poor for real. Survived
in a shed
back of someone else's shack, sweated 365
in a wife-beater.
I subsisted on a graduate stipend and alimony,
on daddy's care packages of soup
and Yuban instant coffee.

One year out of a dead marriage I lived
trying to get back to any body.
AIDs was not yet in the dictionary.
D.H. Lawrence topped my
reading list. *Women in Love.*

Six nights (I wrote "sex nights")
into narrow sleep
on his cot, I found dirt
less Romantic.
Laundry and junk food, unsexy.
When I dropped him, Dennis
waxed tender.
For slumming, I will likely come back
        as striped fur skittering
        across the last dirt road
        in Princeton, flattened
        by a sleep-deprived guy
        whose brakes
        will fail him.

MORE LIKE ME

No, he said, you should write
an important poem, a serious take
on race, sexism and powerful
men. Craft lines that are subtle,
concise, elliptical. Splash less color. Think steel
girders. Less laughter,
no small animals. Forge
gender-bending poems about good-looking
dudes who
read *Sister Carrie* on the A Train.

Skewer politicians.
Take on the plight of fast-food workers,
growth hormones in chicken,
the struggle of Afghan women,
but do not whine like the women
I have pissed on, he said.
Ditch personal politics, go big,
Stop quoting Rich and Piercy.
"Watch who they beat and who they eat,
the rest is decoration."

Decorate my ass!
Write poems more like mine,
he said. Never publish them.
Self-promotion is unfeminine.
You must be contained,
restrained, self-demeaning.
Also younger and prettier.
Have some work done.
Keep your work in the dark.
Write for immortality.

You should write less often, perhaps,
poems with less estrogen,
more balls and gravitas.
But I will never read them.

OFTEN
(*With thanks to Robert Duncan*)

Often in a meadow I hear footsteps—
then I call my therapist or the cops.
No meadows on our block, just
the gated "community" at Harrison Keepe.
They keep riffraff poets like me
out of the park.

Growing up in Rockville Centre,
closest thing to a meadow
was the wooded tract
where the "bum" lived.
1958, that's what our parents
called him. "Homeless" wasn't
on our working-class horizon.

Caren and I were lured by
the seedy lot. Maybe
Freud was right, maybe
sex and death thrived
in that hut raised with
ripped branches.
We aimed to play there.
I was eight, one year away
from "being a woman."
Yep, those days we ate
chickens with more hormones
than Liz Taylor.
We bled young.

My mother read aloud
Growing Up
and Liking It—like, what choice
did I have?

Mommy wrapped our leftovers
for the "vagrant" in the shack,
dropped them on the sidewalk
at wood's edge. Maybe that's what
I want to think, wrap myself a pretend
memory to eat later.

By now the "woods" have been cleared
for condos.
The bum is
a homeless guy and the
Nassau County cops have given
his descendants a long ride
to another county
with fewer hybrids
or taxpayers.

The chickens are leaner.
They listen to NPR.
Really.
A farmer told me
that steady voices
help them to lay
more eggs, to feel
less abandoned. Like footsteps
in a meadow when there are no more
meadows and those before us
have gone, and ashes don't leave footsteps.

Though I often see my mother,
and she's still angry with me.
She lit up when I raved,
"You look good, Ma!"
Bared her jawbone
when I asked her what it's like
being dead.

She blinks the oven light
when she disapproves of something I've
said. Twice a day, on average.
Growing up and liking it!
Oy! Call the exorcist.

THE DIFFERENCE BETWEEN ENVY AND JEALOUSY

Probably my inability
to listen to Billy Collins
is envy, but
it doesn't hit me
with a pang, *au contraire*,
I feel calmer, immersed
in tepid water
like a child. My
mother's hand is
missing, and there's
a sudden draft—the
cold shoulder of
adulthood. Probably
I should thank Billy
Collins—even
the word "mother"
is consolation.

I can picture the
bath, my baby sister
and Mommy's arms,
though they only briefly
reach for me.
I will never be
Poet Laureate

of anything, not even
my mother's heart. So
this is jealousy.
Come to Momma.
No, not you! She
calls her fair
blue-eyed daughter.

Calm down, the poem says,
what more do you
have to lose?
Let the lines
suffice. Little waves.
Let the song
bathe you now.

PASSIONATE

Her breasts were twins
for him. He was dashing in his
uniform, Army Private First Class,
Maxwell Air Force Base,
Montgomery.
Racism was in
then. Another fervent
bridge
between them.
My mother loathed "coloreds."
Daddy feared "schvartzers."

I've written
the uplifting narrative
of how my mother changed
over the years. Living in New York
turned her around.
At 80, in Montgomery,
she took to the streets
in civil-rights protests
against the cancellation
of mid-town buses,
with placards
and young black men.
She stopped being afraid.

Edifying, right?
Those other years,
when fear and hatred bonded
my parents
with almost erotic
energy—
what name does bigotry take
on a chart
of family history?

How to wipe that curse
off the map
without canceling
my birth?

DREAM WITNESS

After the Goodfella wasted me
I played dead. The thug
swaggered like a ham actor,
Soprano understudy.
Now he's plugging
Chik-fil-A.

At last, my turn
to grill the witness:
"Why shoot me?"
We aimed to nail you
when you were young,
when your father
ratted on Joey Gallo
about vending machines
and phone threats.
Fucking wiretaps!
Then bullets
at Umberto's Clam House.

"So? Why send an actor
to whack me
after all these years?"
Crime's an art, too,
Sweetheart.
Some art is a crime.
"Not mine, I hope?"
You know best what's
malformed.

Maybe playing dead
is my crime?
Rise, timid poet!
The Goodfella gets paid scale.

He'll go home,
put his feet up.
Write on louder,
blare like a
brass band. Behind you
marches the house band,

Benny G and
Louie Armstrong,
still knocking 'em dead.
Maybe Joy Harjo will
back you live on sax.
You breathe, you play,
belt out a new song.
Your choice, doll.
Your parade.

"Yes, but how are you different
from the gangsters?"
an academic asked.
"I don't stalk little girls
on the way home
from school.
Don't murder,
don't own a gun.
I write love poems,
not to Joey Gallo.
Leave that to Bobby Dylan.

I don't threaten
anyone,
not at my age.
No animals were smoked
in the making
of this poem."

BIG LOVE

I need to love my herniated disc—it's mine
now, and the fall I took to win it
I own in my low back, L4, L5.
"We were born of a great spiral," Margo said,
and I dove right in.
I'll dedicate my crash landing to the Planetary Genius
Suroth, patron of adolescent love charms.
None of the South Side boys loved us, but Caren and I
fell for each other.
Instead of parents, best friends,
Mango Sherbet lipstick and amulets.

Praise the past, from which we shape
necklaces and songs
to ward off dark.
Praise darkness.
My mother waits there.
Need to relearn birth,
to embrace her.
By now her mean streak
will have burned off.
And Daddy? Will he show?
I'd be his mother now. Once I saw him cry.
Broken rib. I tried to
perch on his knee. "I'm sorry!" he wept.

I want to bless the breaks, the falls,
love gone wrong. No love is wasted,
they say. Spurned love
enriches our soil.
Let us cut back
dead stalks.

Praise open coffins
that teach us not to have one.
Now that we're here,
praise the coffee can they planted my father in.
Dad used to mail me instant Yuban.
Praise my mother for burying his ashes
on a whim.

Praise her coldness.
She tried to "warm us up"
with cocoa and Marshmallow Fluff.
Praise Grandma, who couldn't heat
a can of baby peas.
Weren't we lucky to
have survived childhood!

Praise relearning
to walk.
Praise balance and
my spine that yells at me.
Praise poems with backbone.

Praise our friends who hold us up,
and our former friends
who have abandoned us.

Praise karma.
Praise the step I tripped on.
Praise Dante who built stairs,

and God who built Dante.
Praise Beatrice.
Praise Joan Rivers.

Praise the Long Island Expressway,
where I spent my childhood
in the back seat of the Studebaker
my father brought home from the lot.
Praise used-car salesmen,
traffic and stalling.
Praise soft-serve cones, time out
from misery.
Praise childhood,
whatever our parents handed us,
or couldn't.

Praise our children
who teach us humility.
Praise crawling, tantrums
and plastic spoons.
Praise the love that feeds us,
the love we take into our bodies,
and love we will never have.

Praise holding on,
grasping fingers
and free-fall,
the sacred mountains
we glimpse
when we jump up,
the panoramic
spill
when we
let go.

ODE TO A PETAL ON THE RIVERBANK

You are peeled off,
past. "How long are you
going to keep doing this?"
the white-haired man at the
back of the room mocked, at
the Baptist College reading.
"As long as I have breath, Sir!"

I didn't say, "You should talk,
Old-Timer!
Double standard, anyone?"
Or, "I don't know. Poetry won't
make me young again,
won't make him
love me." (O Hank Williams,
you back-seat driver!)

Sweet petal,
still kissed by the
Mediterranean
sun, your mouth
offers color I have never seen
at home—purple rouge,
silky light. If I owned this dress
I would wear it every day
and no one would ask,
"How long?"
What choice, o mortals, do
we have?

We can love
despite no-love,
despite
mind-numbing news,
despite Dallas, Nice,

Baton Rouge.
You don't have to be pretty
to love, you
don't have to be young.
"Love that has no hope
of love," like Nureyev
in the mind, pirouetting
toward Sleeping Beauty.
"It's not so bad,"
he says, twirling her
offstage.

The bruised petal
no longer
argues. She
enters the grainy idiom
of earth,
humming herself back
into the banks
of the Seine,
the Tennessee,
the Garonne.

WHEN

the low heavy sky weighs down like a cast-iron skillet,
there's nothin' cookin', Chuck.

When my ancient neighbor told me that his cat Ophelia
was old, I chimed, "So am I!" He jumped back.

"*Ah non!*" he gasped, one tooth in his mouth.
Who can afford dentistry in a medieval village?

Women should not be old. Slick petals
on the cobblestones flaunt

pink, rouge, coral,
and it doesn't seem fair

that those we step on hold allure.
Ophelia's not worried. She climbs from the sill

to the motorcycle, *sans souci.* I bet
that warm leather seat feels good.

I am jealous of a cat. Ages
since anyone took me for a ride.

I was eighteen, leaned the wrong way.
Tommy sped me back to my dorm.

Still left-leaning, I watch from my window,
tune a forbidden song at seventy,

ache with the best of them, athletic
        in my yearning.

ALTERNATIVE

To those who prefer rivers over regrets,
I recommend the Garonne,
Steely one moment,

Olive the next.
Still and then
Rushing to swallow

All the sorrows young women
Have bundled
In—goodbyes to infants, to

Treacherous men.
The truth? The river is no less
Treacherous than love, some days

It too swells, monstrous.
Then history is not your friend.
Try amnesia and

Wave after wave of love—
One may restore
Your pearl.

Today the green water
Barely trembles.
Step in.

COMMON

We held so much in common—desire,
though you longed for someone

else, and I was someone else but not
that one, not young.

Bodies, we both had them, and
yearned.

We loved Neruda and Kay Ryan.
What else? Scotch.

I poured Lagavulin or
Dark Storm.

We both loved you and your beauty,
so fierce that your neck

cracked trying to bear up
under it.

By the end, I needed an exorcism.
You enacted your own.

Taught me what love is
without a body. Why lyrics

compare it to the moon
and sun.

Some loves are not about lips.
Poems emerge

from them.
Consolation.

ENCORE
After Eluard

I love you for all the men I do not love
and for those I adore,

for the crackle of croissants
and the perfume of escargots,

for *Macho Macho Man*
at Café St. Victor

and the snobs
at Librairie Compagnie,

for les *chats françaises*
et les *chats américains*,

for all the Frenchmen whose beauty
tossed in olive oil

cannot equal the taste of yours.
I love you to love.

I love you for your silences,
but I prefer your songs.

I love you for your wisdom,
mostly in your arms.

Tell me who you haunt
and I'll tell you who you are.

You haunt me like a summer hit.
Replay me on your lips.

I love you for all the wine
I have not tasted.

I love you to stay drunk
on love,

Like Baudelaire and Arthur,
but breathing.

III. *How Our Bodies Learned*

MOTH LIGHT

Some things are not funny.
The oven flared, we two

Inside. Sudden stab
Of heat and then

Even though we are masters
Of transformation

The blinding light
Went blank.

We had heard humans
Did this to each other.

Why us, fragile
And harmless as silk?

Why ignite our fanning
Orbit

Around the fickle
Sun?

HOW OUR BODIES LEARNED ABOUT FLINT

Knoxville, Tennessee

1.
At last the guy from HEP plumbing arrives
to save our screwed septic system.
We have no water, only
the word "water." Sewage backs up
in the downstairs tub.
I think "Flint, Michigan,"
thank God it's
not us.

No comparison, of course.
We run filtered drinking water.
We own the least impressive house
in upscale Riverbend,
but the river doesn't bend its lead into our
tap. I think "Flint," love the sound,
the stony fire-starter *clink*, hate callous
politicians. We can't drink Flint, but we
raise a toast (with bottled water),
with poems that offer
stopgap sips, hopes
for clean cascades.

We're not Flint
on Blueridge Drive, but now
we've had a mouthful. We can't bathe
in our own muck,
or wash our clothes. This murky mess
at least helps us imagine,
taste—don't swallow!—and see.

2.
When I turned five, the water monster was
fluoride.
The John Birch Society claimed
Communists were out
to sink us through our taps.
I trudged home from the
dentist's on Sunrise. More cavities, drilling,
drilling. No anesthetic. 1951,
Ike was teaching us
to tough it out.
Children didn't feel pain.
Daddy sold used Caddys
and rattletraps.
No bonuses
for numbing.

At home, we gulped cherry Kool-Aid
from jelly glasses.
Jonestown and metaphor
hadn't been
invented. We snarfed down Wonder Bread,
canned pineapple,
Spam,
first and secondhand smoke.

3.
But this is not about 1950's,
child welfare,
ignorance or poverty.
This is about current lead levels
in the blood of Flint's children.
Their developing
brains.

"The EPA now declares the water is 'safe enough'
for children and pregnant women."

"There may be no threshold
for developmental effects of lead
on children."

Risk factors
for lead poisoning:
Living in a developmental country.
Living in Flint, Michigan.
Living in East Chicago.
Living in poverty,
in black neighborhoods
in the United States.

4.
CNN tracked one Flint family
that used 151 bottles of water
in a month.
As long as you can afford to be pure,
you'll be fine.
And for bathing?
Don't worry, the EPA says.
Dust and toys cause more problems
than water.

Drink up!
Scotch,
if you can afford it.
Joke about why Jesus changed water
into wine.

Note to the press: Don't use "miscarriage"
as metaphor, as in "miscarriage
of justice," in the same article

where Flint's women claim
that drinking water
wasted
their unborn.

When Flint officials shifted the supply
from Detroit Water to Flint River,
a tributary "notorious for its filth
due to the presence of fecal coliform
bacteria,"
what did they think?
Thought they would save money.
"Water is deemed safe but parents
of young children are advised
to consult with their doctors."

"Lead levels almost double
what is considered toxic."
December, 2016, only two per cent
of 30,000 underground lead pipes
have been replaced
in Flint.

City official Mike Glascow says he was ordered to
alter water quality reports,
remove the highest lead levels.

Safe? It's "safe enough."
We know where the real filth lies.

MOVE OVER, CATULLUS

I hate & I
love. Brother,
you're not the
only one.
When I live
in the shadow
of his silences,
I hate like an ink-infested
squid in a squeeze.

When he speaks
I'm a viable human.
Me, a feminist
for god's sake,
no man's island!
So how did this
compressed want
become my
globe?

Sorcery!
He's Circe,
though he looks
like Rob Lowe.
I'm beached,
I tell you.
Sand in my mouth.
Once a month

He fucking "likes"
My post. Too little
too late, mate.
Unspell me!
Un-sorcel my brain.
I hate and I

love. Star swirl.
Pick me out of the line-up
of the love-struck
and put me back
on my planet.
I'll hate
injustice, intolerance,
real blows. Then
hating will be
a way of loving him.

OUT

Out of order
& we know it,
the body's been left behind
without a scream.

The world wavers in front of us,
all the bright white houses waver
as if seen through smoke or water,
our eyes are unsure.

Soft, this is all we have,
grandmothers and wolves,
our eyes to see the bigger with,
our mouths, the better, at least,
to say no with.

But if, after so many mouths
our words are shot in back
of the tongue?

If, after so many cries,
our silence also comes to waste us?

WARRIOR SONG, AFTER BREXIT
(June 25, 2016)

Trump's gloating over torn Europe like a fat orange guppy
      with hair. "My children can't stop crying,"
a London poet wrote. Long ago Heather called
      from her room, "I can't sleep, Mommy!
      The trees are crying." Hacked for starter castles,
the oaks slammed down. Judas redbuds
      with heart-shaped leaves shuttled
      broken-off in trash bags.
"You can't leave the poem there," a young poet says. I taught
      his class a Dakota song:
      "You cannot harm me.
      You cannot harm one
      who has dreamed a dream like mine."
Now I wrap myself
in dream songs, chant through the halls of our ivory tower.
      Europe is crumbling like a biscuit.
      The tyrant blusters,
      eating it up. Fear's his favorite breakfast.
"You cannot harm me," the warrior sang.
      Young poet asks, "How did that work out?"
Pretty ending would be
      the new lie.
(November 9, 2016)
      Now, breaks-it is on us.
U.S.
      We don't want to leave the house,
bed,
      bottle.

Outside the library
      our students
raise signs: "No Rapist for Prez!"
      Two p.m., a Trump thug punched

Jazmin's friend in the face.
          "They called us 'niggers!'"
Mona said. She called in sick
          yesterday.

Normal now to be sick-afraid, but we
          need to circle the hurt,
          be cells that speak to each other
in one new body.
          We'll find each other, easy
with "Not My President!" signs.
          We'll rebuild. Speak out.
          We know fear won't protect us.
Silence can't cure. *So it is better to*
          speak, our friend Audre said.
Jazmin, take my hand.
One by one and by twos,
          together we'll clear the air.
          Our children will laugh
at the myth of an orange gob who
          bullied his way to
power. They'll howl
          at an orange buffoon.
          Even in the future, he will hate the sound
of their laughter.

Wiccans, we beg you: bind him
to his own voice, deafen
and defeat him.
By his own will, he is bound
to a white sheet
and orange toupee.

Bind him in
the hell of his own making,
Bedtime for Bonzo,
part two.

Unbind we-the-people,
from this wild
boar who is tearing up
the graves of our ancesters
and the future of green earth.

WAKE ME (AFTER ORLANDO)
by Marilyn Kallet and Benjamin McClendon

I want to wake and find I'm dreaming.
Want to wake up and find
I'm human. But Trump
blares hatred,
and I'm not dead yet.

Why are casings common
as nutshells? News anchors inform us
they blow in on the wind, and this
is the story we are supposed to believe:
thirty percent chance of bullets,
mostly sunny skies, massacre
front moving through this Sunday.

Nutshells, nut jobs,
sounds harmless, but
now we are all watching our steps
and backs. Winds are sharper
than tanned forecasters led us
to believe. Those casings scatter
more plentiful than seed.
We can't beg God to stop this, too slow.

We have to intervene, grow
more human, turn this cyclone
around. Return to sender: fear
trumpeted by Donald
and his shellacked minions.
We can't swallow shells and survive.

We hold names of the innocent
on our lips. Teach fathers
to speak more of mercy,
less of Judgement.

We are the fathers, and now
the mothers, sisters and brothers
burying our dead.

No stirring the newsfeed
to nightmare because we're already
there, afraid to gather,
afraid to leave the house
when we're already pinching
ourselves, each other,
pressing our eyes closed
fast as we can.

A pinch of salt preserves
the dead, one more
lessens bitterness, pinch
of salt in the soil is all it takes
to kill the seeds, to dry up fields
for a hundred years. Somewhere

we can dig down to fresh water,
but not in the basement. Somewhere
streams an answer to the thirst
that dries our mouths
to silence. Somehow we must find
strength to step outside again.

(*After June 13, 2016*)

ANTI-BULLET ADULT

"Be an anti-bullet adult!" the DJ said. "Help one child."
Great, I said, I'm in! Here's my chance to stand up
Against guns.

Then I heard, "anti-bullying adult." Oh.
I want that, too.
Where's the door that lets me in

To the anti-bullet room?
I want to be the adult.
Want to stop the gun madness here.

I don't care about Uncle Herbie
With his gun-rights rant.
Don't care about Heidi's guy

With his gun locker in Dunwoody.
"Guns are his toys," she sighed.
I'm lying. I do care.

This is my family.
I don't want to fear
My own well-armed family.

ANTI-BULLET, #2
   (San Bernardino, 12/5/2015)

I became "baby girl."
My name
Changed to Abandoned.

My name
Burst
Grandma's tears.

Mommy's arms
Were the other kind.
The taste of metal,

Not milk.
Call me
Dead End.

Reporters snapped photos
Of my toys.
Anderson Cooper scowled.

Reporters!
Even tragedy is good for someone.
Not for me.

ANTI-BULLET, #3
(San Bernardino, 12/5/2015)

Without a throat,
I couldn't swallow. Packing light,
I once spoke pickpockets,
Prison guards,
My uncle in Murder Incorporated.
But I couldn't spell the mother
Who dumped her baby
For bullets.

"I have been things worse than any
I have seen," Rosicrucians say.
But I have not been that mother
Whose baby became cover,
A front for bullets.
I am an anti-bullet human.
Emptiness where song
Should be.

Something's stuck,
The letter N.
No no no.
The sound of an infant
Pining. The
Sound of choking
On rage that
Smelled of flesh,
Blood, metal blinding.

NO
    "No one has come forward to say they saw this coming."
    Police Chief Burguan, San Bernardino, April 10, 2017.

No
NO!
Bigger each time, upside down
eye chart.

Two adults and one child dead, but
the special-needs children
of North Park Elementary
"were not targeted," the news says.
Breathing children were
bussed to other campuses,
given light sticks
to play with.

"My son was targeted the moment
the state made it legal to carry
a gun. My son was targeted
the moment the NRA opened their
bank account."

Words matter less to the kids than
service dogs, who let themselves
be cuddled, and don't ask.
Tell the children we will protect them,
the protocol advises.
"The bad man has a twin
and he'll be back," one child cried.

Karen Elaine Smith was a special ed teacher,
ten years at North Park.
Her ex was pissed off.
Domestic violence is not news.
Reporters gasped when they learned

eight-year-old Jonathan Martinez
had died.

My sister who counsels survivors
was six
when a guy threatened
Daddy
and our family.
Police escorted her
to Oceanside School Number 5.
She saw the figure five in red.
Did she have PTSD
in 2017 when Breitbart posted her name
on a hit-list of civil servants
Trump could get rid of?
This is no longer a poem about metaphor,
or someone else's house.
Marshalls installed a panic button
under her desk. "Is your home
secure?" they asked.

Armed men
target women
and children first.
IPV,
intimate partner violence.
Not news, it will kill you.

Button your lips
if you're a federal employee.
"Threats are normal,"
Homeland says.
You can still cry.
Sherlock, the Police Chief's canine,
is the fur person
kids at North Park want near them.
Sherlock tosses like a rug with eyes.

Warm-blooded,
he doesn't run for office.
Easier to hug
than a White House wreath.

TOO SOON, ZAEVION

In memory of Zaevion Dobson, killed by gunfire in
Knoxville, 12/17/2015

A fifteen-year-old should be
Dreaming about prom,
Whom to invite,

About football,
Number 24, sprinting
To the end line,

About classes,
Colleges,
About anything.

But Zaevian Dobson
Hurled his strong
Young body

In the way of bullets.
His body was too human
To shatter metal.

His body proved
Strong enough to stop bullets
From killing two friends,

Young women who will
Embody his memory
Long as they live.

Maybe they will call
A son
Zaevion, and tell him,

"You are named for
a man who was not too young
to do the right thing. A hero."

"Yes, yes, we know,"
teens will sigh.
President Obama invoked him,

The young man who
Sacrificed himself
Without a breath of doubt.

But I am thinking now of Mrs. Dobson,
His mother, who taught him
To think first

Of others,
Thinking of the ache,
The emptiness,

Her son
Shattered by cold metal
Fired from the hands

Of twenty-somethings:
"barrage of bullets"
"senseless shooting spree"—

As if there could be
A meaningful shooting
spree—

Zaevion is a beautiful name,
Now more beautiful,
His mother's consolation.

A tenth-grader,
He should have been
Studying biology

And playing ball.
He should still be
Home with family.

Aren't I a mother too?
So I lay my heart on the page
For Mrs. Dobson.

I want to kill the bullet that
Killed your son, Zenobia.
Want to stop this madness.

Would I throw myself in the way?
I am a professor,
But Zae is my teacher now.

PRAISE

Praise this day's soggy greyness,
and every day,
overcast bastards and blue reprieves.

Solitary days in Auvillar,
useless unless you count
a few lines of poetry

and cats in the windows.
Tonight I will meet friends
and our words will clasp

like dancers in the streets,
for Saint Noé.
There will be wine.

Praise the grey day that leads to the
delights of evening.
No great love will wait for me on the doorstep.

Friendship holds its consolations.
What I wouldn't give to see your face.
Passersby with black umbrellas don't make a comment

on my life. We seek cover
where we can.
A mockingbird trills behind bricks of Carolingian walls.

Praise birdsong, praise notes of missing you that
underscore my life, day by day.
If my praise doesn't touch you, maybe it will

tap someone else,
like incessant rain on sandy earth.
Monsieur Claude has dug his garden and something red

and juicy
waits to yield,
drinking it all in.

HARD LOVE

You were the jazz I
never got to hear—

distance
with a body

a perfect body—
I touched it

with my lines. So?
You were the night sky

and black holes.
You were the

space
between

between.
Hard love? Impossible.

Eve turned
gap-toothed

when she bit
the hardest apple.

Good news/bad:
On the 7th day,

God created
you, single malt,

& the hard-hearted
hard-bodied

blues.

LOSING IT
"The universe is absent from all your plans"
(Gérard de Nerval)

Somewhere at the Atlanta airport
I dropped *Diabetes with Owls*—my signed

Sedaris—tucked inside, a fat
missive from Marge Piercy about traffic

wrecks, the Boston bombing, cozy
sleeping cars, her slope of daffodils.

I believed her letter would save me
from falling out of air. Reread it

a hundred times. Good thing,
now it's only in my brain.

As my friend Alice said about losing love,
"It was like swallowing a couch."

Or a hardback,
with a voucher for paradise inside.

Quickly I bought another Sedaris,
the way we Americans shop double

when we feel like Job,
spilled my woes

to the young African-American
bookstore clerk with the tee-shirt logo:

My Story's Worse!
"Oh no! A signed copy!"

"But think of it this way—
someone else has found treasure!"

Then I boarded Air France and
eight hours and one

supposedly *saumon parmentier* later,
at Charles DeGaulle, my loss

seemed lighter,
a bubble with a feather on it.

Those missing pages sailed in front of me,
out of sight, with my early dead.

My father in his GI khakis
did not look up. The top of his handsome

dark head gleamed with Bryl Cream, in lines
his little black comb had drawn.

In Atlanta I had sworn to write more, to patch
rips in the fabric of in my existence

with poetry, never again to lose mindlessly.
Not to bargain with God.

When I woke two days later in Auvillar,
strips of duck breast sizzling in the skillet,

a bowl of yogurt flavored with violet figs
set on my table, I was calm.

My belly pooched out
Buddha-like,

and I felt less stricken
by what a bobblehead I am.

Lost and found seemed *pareil*, equal,
as if I had caught some

particulate in my net
worth more than the Piercy letter

which will perhaps
pop up on eBay

along with the Chanukah book
I once signed—*L'Chayim!*—to John Updike.

LONGEST NIGHT: RECITAL FOR ORGAN AND VIOLIN
St. Pierre, Auvillar

1.
Grey stone and freezing benches
after a day of
worrying
a blast of sound

sweeps me
to memory—
my young daughter on vibes
now I'm solo

in this church surging
Led Zeppelin gone Bach
Uh oh the
music grows agitated

organ frenzied &
pounding—
villagers arrive
& we need to

give them time
to be unfriendly
in a friendly
kind of way.

2.
A day trashed
by stress
my only words
a letter to

Sedaris
penned at the salon
where Annie
angrily pulled my hair

& then I
overtipped her
(My right as
an American!)

Now the Franco-German society
lets go of Jews and guilt
for a mo,
shifts to

rock
pulverised
for violin
& *orgue*

Procol Harum?
Really?
Jesus is looking
down

on the violin.
I could pick up
an old person
tonight.

3.
Tous les enfants
sont
endormis—
sleeping

in the arms of
schmaltz.
The villagers
seem puzzled

by "A Whiter Shade of Pale."
Maybe if we could
slow-dance
with Jules Schwartz

before he got his
braces—but
this is church,
for God's sake

not Oceanside
School #5.
Boring can be
transcendental.

What if
I pass out
and fall off
the church bench

onto the stone floor?
Will Pink Floyd
go on?
You can tell

the violinist
would be great
if he was playing
actual music.

4.
Old guy staring at me—
foreplay?
Should I take up
with the Lesser Cheeseman?

These thoughts
descend
during
"Stairway to Heaven."

Agnes wants to
sleep with Violin Man
because of his "perfect
intonation."

Wait!
Is that Jesus
in a rowboat?
With dolphins?

Shine On You
Crazy Diamond.
Gerhard in
flipflops

the violinist
in Sixties jeans
Oy!
Your own concert

you couldn't put on
a decent pair of pants?
Now it's the
"Sound of Silence"

I wish!
Jesus up there
swaddled in
a giant baby

blanket
like a larva
cherubim
tug on him

his hands thrown
like
Nu, What did you
expect?

Before we rush the exit
Marie-José
passes
the hat.

FAILED ODE TO ABSENCE

Always
where, and you,
plein air.

My words
seek you
across

oceans,
time zones.
I wanted to

write
an ode to
absence,

but you,
love,
got in the way.

      No poem
without you
      in the square
where I was cruel
      to you
      years ago.
I want to take
      back my words,
beg the wind:
      rush the dark-haired
poet
      back to me!

But the gale
        turns no, cold
shoulder.

It will whip
through this
square

in Moissac
for centuries
after us.

The mistral
has no need
of love,

turns its back,
like you.
I toss words

like coins
into a fountain.
Maybe a curious child

will find one,
warm it
in his hands.

"What power has love
but forgiveness?"
This power, love,

to start again.
The wind surges
through my lines,

doesn't care
about age,
vows.

This gust
of song
belongs to us.

One day
it will wrap
our voices

in silky sounds
and quiet,
in time.

OLD SUN

The sun that shuddered on my past
trembles this morning.
If Orpheus is the sun,

he's not disguised.
His hair burns grey ash,
shorter but

those eyes those
fierce lips—
he should be hiding.

Why do I keep finding him?
He's on my Profile,
& sometimes I view myself

as him, giving me
the illusion
he's participating

in our love.
"Our" would be like
waking

to find
the flower of having passed
through Paradise

in my hand.

EDEN AGAIN

All the salt was spent on icy roads.
The last poem loves the road

to the lake, to the husband and the daughter
who plans her own wedding.

The last poem is a cleansing,
letting go until

there can be no
turning. "He is not your friend,"

a friend said. "I don't know what he is."
He's his own man, complete, a wrap.

The last poem doesn't wave
or waiver,

opens a chapter
embodied

all the way
to ash.

Lot does not look back.
His wife keeps her own

secret name.
She's spicy,

no regrets.
"Come here," she says.

And he stops being old.
Cradles her breasts

in his hands,
and no fruit is forbidden.

BAD FRENCH LIP-READING, MORNING MASS

(Auvillar, 22 mai, 2016,
Fête de la Saint Noé)

Before the alpaca,
There was Jesus coffee,
God in all things.
In houses
Named February.
"What's he doing in the
Center of the cross?"

In Calypso
There's a saying:
"I am in the pot."
Let's make confiture.
We must open the fists
Of our hearts.
Outside, no swords.

For those who hide
In marriage,
For journalists and victims
Of Oedipus, bless them.
Son of the internet,
Grease them.
To all men who have lost their clothes:

In the apple tree of blood,
Make jam.

TURNING

"You're tedious,"
a voice said (someone
substantial sd

I knew it was swimaway
time
—in

a river of light.
"You're Jewish,"
someone

said.
Light tasted
sweet,

I turned,
river—light
knew me,

tasted
me.

MUSE

After Eluard and Breton

I love you for your
black ink
hair your
words of earth &
iron your
body of
flesh &
stone your
A-line
strict lines I love
you for all the time
we will never make love
for the years between
us for your silences
which are wounds
for your songs that are balm.

I love you for night
and shadow
coffee and dawn
a touch of cream
a bowl of gold
cherries,
for the
mystery
of never
having you
I love you to love
if you turned
my way
I would be scorched,
wordless.

No, I promise
I will find my song
of earth
fire
and wine,
tasting you always
for the very first time.

NOTES

"What power has love but forgiveness?" This epigraph and refrain ("Failed Ode to Absence") comes from William Carlos Williams' great love poem, "Asphodel, That Greeny Flower," first published in *Journey to Love*, Random House, 1955.

"Kitchen Rag" opens with an epigraph by French-Lebanese author Vénus Khoury-Ghata; her poem appears in the anthology *Couleurs Femmes*, Le Castor Astral, 2010.

"What I Never Had" includes two lines from Robert Duncan's "Variations on Two Dicta of William Blake," *Roots and Branches*, 1964.

"Retreat" holds phrases from Adrienne Rich's "Translations," *Diving Into the Wreck*, W.W. Norton, 1973.

"How Our Bodies Learned About Flint": The shift from Detroit Water and Sewage (DWSD) to the Flint River occurred on April 25, 2014. NPR quotes the mayor's press release: "'It's regular, good, pure drinking water, and it's right in our backyard,' said Mayor [Dayne] Walling." As for treating the pipes to prevent possible lead contamination, the city took a "wait-and-see approach," according to Michigan Radio. http://www.npr.org/sections/thetwo-way/2016/04/20/465545378/lead-laced-water-in-flint-a-step-by-step-look-at-the-makings-of-a-crisis

Researchers have long known the damaging effects on children's brains of even low-level lead exposure. For example, see "Intellectual Impairment in Children with Blood Lead Concentrations Below 10 μg Per Deciliter," April 17, 2003: http://www.nejm.org/doi/full/10.1056/NEJMoa022848#t=article

"Flint water deemed safe..." "Lead levels almost double..." CNN has tracked the water crisis and the corruption of officials in Flint, Michigan: http://www.cnn.com/2016/03/04/us/flint-water-crisis-fast-facts/index.html

"For the record, Flint is 57% black, 37% white, 4% Latino and 4% mixed race; more than 41% of its residents live below the poverty level, according to the U.S. Census. NAACP President and CEO Cornell Brooks drew a direct connection between Flint's socioeconomic factors and the toxic drinking water. 'Environmental Racism + Indifference = Lead in the Water & Blood,' he tweeted." Michael Martinez, "Flint, Michigan, Did Race and Poverty Factor into the Water Crisis?" CNN, 11:16 AM, January 28, 2016. http://www.cnn.com/2016/01/26/us/flint-michigan-water-crisis-race-poverty/index.html.

"When" opens with a riff on Baudelaire's "Spleen": "*Quand le ciel bas et lourd pèse comme un couvercle*" (When the low heavy sky weighs down like a lid"). *Les Fleurs du Mal*, 1857.

"Encore" echoes Paul Eluard's "Je t'aime," *Le Phénix*, 1951; reprinted with my translation in *Last Love Poems of Paul Eluard*, Black Widow Press, 2006, 145.

"Wake Me, After Orlando" is a collaborative poem with Benjamin McClendon, who is a doctoral student in creative writing/poetry at the University of Tennessee. His poems have appeared in *Rattle*, *Blue Fifth Review*, among other journals.

"Muse" takes up Eluard's refrain from "*Je t'aime*," and closes with a play on Breton's "*Toujours pour la première fois*" ("Always for the first time"), 1934.

MARILYN KALLET is the author of 17 previous books, including *The Love That Moves Me* and *Packing Light: New and Selected Poems,* poetry from Black Widow Press. She has translated Paul Eluard's *Last Love Poems,* Péret's *The Big Game,* and co-translated Chantal Bizzini's *Disenchanted City.* Dr. Kallet is Nancy Moore Goslee Professor of English at the University of Tennessee. She leads poetry workshops every year for VCCA-France in Auvillar. She has performed her poems on campuses and in theaters across the United States as well as in France and Poland, as a guest of the U.S. Embassy's "America Presents" program. The University of Tennessee has listed her as a specialist on poetry's role in times of crisis, as well as on poetry and healing, poetry and humor, poetry and dreams, poetry and Jewish identity.

TITLES FROM BLACK WIDOW PRESS
TRANSLATION SERIES

A Life of Poems, Poems of a Life
by Anna de Noailles. Translated by Norman R.
Shapiro. Introduction by Catherine Perry.

Approximate Man and Other Writings
by Tristan Tzara. Translated and edited by
Mary Ann Caws.

Art Poétique by Guillevic.
Translated by Maureen Smith.

The Big Game
by Benjamin Péret. Translated with an
introduction by Marilyn Kallet.

Boris Vian Invents Boris Vian: A Boris Vian Reader.
Edited and translated by Julia Older.

Capital of Pain
by Paul Eluard. Translated by Mary Ann Caws,
Patricia Terry, and Nancy Kline.

Chanson Dada: Selected Poems
by Tristan Tzara. Translated with an introduction
and essay by Lee Harwood.

Earthlight (Clair de Terre)
by André Breton. Translated by Bill Zavatsky and
Zack Rogow. (New and revised edition.)

*Essential Poems and Writings of Joyce Mansour:
A Bilingual Anthology.* Translated with an
introduction by Serge Gavronsky.

Essential Poems and Prose of Jules Laforgue.
Translated and edited by Patricia Terry.

*Essential Poems and Writings of Robert Desnos:
A Bilingual Anthology.* Edited with an introduction
and essay by Mary Ann Caws.

EyeSeas (Les Ziaux) by Raymond Queneau.
Translated with an introduction by Daniela
Hurezanu and Stephen Kessler.

Fables in a Modern Key by Pierre Coran.
Translated by Norman R. Shapiro. Full-color
illustrations by Olga Pastuchiv.

Fables of Town & Country by Pierre Coran.
Translated by Norman R. Shapiro. Full-color
illustrations by Olga Pastuchiv.

*Forbidden Pleasures: New Selected Poems
1924–1949* by Luis Cernuda. Translated by
Stephen Kessler.

Furor and Mystery & Other Writings
by René Char. Edited and translated by Mary Ann
Caws and Nancy Kline.

*The Gentle Genius of Cécile Périn: Selected Poems
(1906–1956).* Edited and translated by
Norman R. Shapiro.

Guarding the Air: Selected Poems of Gunnar Harding.
Translated and edited by Roger Greenwald.

The Inventor of Love & Other Writings
by Gherasim Luca. Translated by Julian & Laura
Semilian. Introduction by Andrei Codrescu. Essay
by Petre Răileanu.

Jules Supervielle: Selected Prose and Poetry.
Translated by Nancy Kline & Patricia Terry.

La Fontaine's Bawdy
by Jean de La Fontaine. Translated with an
introduction by Norman R. Shapiro.

Last Love Poems of Paul Eluard. Translated with an
introduction by Marilyn Kallet.

Love, Poetry (L'amour la poésie) by Paul Eluard.
Translated with an essay by Stuart Kendall.

Pierre Reverdy: Poems, Early to Late.
Translated by Mary Ann Caws and Patricia Terry.

Poems of André Breton: A Bilingual Anthology.
Translated with essays by Jean-Pierre Cauvin and
Mary Ann Caws.

Poems of A.O. Barnabooth by Valery Larbaud.
Translated by Ron Padgett and Bill Zavatsky.

Poems of Consummation by Vicente Aleixandre.
Translated by Stephen Kessler.

Préversities: A Jacques Prévert Sampler.
Translated and edited by Norman R. Shapiro.

The Sea and Other Poems by Guillevic.
Translated by Patricia Terry. Introduction by
Monique Chefdor.

To Speak, to Tell You? Poems by Sabine Sicaud.
Translated by Norman R. Shapiro. Introduction
and notes by Odile Ayral-Clause.

Forthcoming title:
I Have Invented Nothing: Selected Poems
by Jean-Pierre Rosnay. Translated by J. Kates.

MODERN POETRY SERIES

WWW.BLACKWIDOWPRESS.COM